THE TAO OF DEATH

THE TAO OF DEATH

An Adaptation of the Tao Te Ching

KAREN WYATT

The Tao of Death
An Adaptation of the Tao Te Ching
.... By ....
KAREN WYATT

ebook ISBN: 979-8-9861488-8-5

Paperback ISBN: 979-8-9861488-9-2

Sunroom Studios
PO Box 5070
Dillon, CO 80435
Kwyattmd@comcast.net

A Special Invitation:

Get the FREE
Companion Journal

To accompany you through *The Tao of Death* and enhance your learning experience, I have created a **FREE Companion Journal** that you can access online and download immediately. You can use the journal prompts as you contemplate each verse of *The Tao of Death* and record your insights and reflections on the journal pages or in your own notebook. These same prompts are included in the Appendix of this book, but you may want to download the free journal as well to make it easier to write about them.

By using this book and the **Companion Journal** as a daily guide to contemplating Death you will gradually become comfortable with the issues you will face at the end of life and learn how to make the most of every moment of life. Please download the journal and enjoy the journey!

Visit the following page to get free access to your
Companion Journal now:

Eoluniversity.com/journal

INTRODUCTION

"Man ... lives as if he is never going to die, and then dies having never really lived."

This quote from the Dalai Lama is a sad commentary on modern life. How tragic that our desire to live the best **life** ends up failing because we ignore the universal and unalterable truth of **death**. Every living thing ultimately dies. That is an inherent fact on this planet but somehow over the past century it has been rejected and forgotten, all to the detriment of mankind. Our medical system goes to great expense to preserve and prolong life and yet most of us don't even enjoy being alive. In fact a recent Harris Poll found that two thirds of Americans report feeling unhappy with life a majority of the time. So we long for lives that will never end but we don't embrace the lives we have been given.

In contrast however, the tiny country of Bhutan in the Himalayas has been named "the happiest place on Earth" despite being a developing nation lacking in many of the comforts that are taken for granted in the U.S. An even greater contrast is the fact that most Bhutanese people, as part of their Buddhist tradition, practice a ritual of thinking about death five times a day, every day. Rather than avoid the subject of death out of fear, they intentionally prepare themselves for the inevitable transition that each of us will one day face. So confronting the fleeting nature of life does not diminish happiness for the Bhutanese and, in fact, may increase the joy they experience on a daily basis.

IS THERE A CORRELATION BETWEEN THINKING ABOUT DEATH AND FINDING HAPPINESS IN LIFE?

No one knows for sure, but it has been shown that contemplating death and the impermanence of life on a regular basis diminishes fear of the unknown. When fear decreases there is a greater opportunity for the expression of love, joy and happiness in life. In my own experience as a hospice physician I found that my fear of death disappeared after spending hours and hours at the bedsides of dying patients. I learned to focus on the things that are most important to me because life is brief and precious. This awareness changed how I live each moment of my life and brought me incredible joy in the small wonders of existence. In addition I am at peace about my own death and feel prepared to accept it whenever it arrives.

I was not a stranger to death when I began my hospice experience for it had been in my awareness since a young age after my cousin and two friends each died unexpectedly. Later my father's suicide death took me to the depths of grief and gave me an intimate look at loss. Then hospice work broadened my perspective as I was given the opportunity to observe many, many patients and families while they coped with the process of dying. From these experiences the contemplation of death became part of my everyday life and was naturally woven into my spiritual life, as well. As a "medical mystic" I was already integrating a spiritual perspective into my healing work with patients and I found that meditations on death fit perfectly into that paradigm.

The greatest lesson to learn from the contemplation of death is that life is precious *because* it is brief and fleeting. When we know that we could die at any moment we are less likely to squander our time and resources. We connect more deeply with our loved ones and enjoy the small miracles of life more fully when we don't know how much longer that opportunity will be available to us. Embracing death, it turns out, is actually the secret to living a life of greater meaning and depth, even though that wisdom might sound contradictory. Death represents the doorway to a full life, not the absence of meaning as we may have believed.

As we struggle with numerous challenges on planet Earth and face the possibility of total annihilation, now is the time to both wake up and face up to death. Now we must embrace this secret pathway through suffering, loss and the unknown in order to find the true meaning of life and our own true purpose within this existence. This is the time when we can no longer afford the luxury of ignoring death and pretending that we are immortal. Now we must face the reality of our finite physical bodies and use this knowledge to fuel our growth in consciousness and spirituality.

WHY ADAPT THE *TAO TE CHING*?

In my spiritual studies I have long cherished the approach of Eastern philosophy to both life and death, including Lao Tzu's *Tao Te Ching*. This little book of wisdom is beloved in China and thought to have been written in the fifth century BCE, though almost nothing is known about Lao Tzu himself. Over the years since my first introduction to the *Tao Te Ching* I have read many different translations and adaptations, always marveling at the relevance of these ancient verses to modern settings.

Translator Stephen Mitchell describes the *Tao Te Ching* (meaning the Book of the Way) as "the classic manual on the art of living, and one of the wonders of the world. ... [It] looks at the basic predicament of being alive and gives advice that imparts balance and perspective, a serene and generous spirit."

As I contemplated the current dismal state of end-of-life care in the Western world and wondered how to lessen our rampant fear of death, an epiphany came to me: why not interpret ancient wisdom for today's readers through the lens of death? In this way I could combine my own two passions for spiritual wisdom and death awareness and create verses that might help others face the reality of dying and death. This book began as an experiment but quickly grew into an inspirational piece filled with such profound wisdom that it had to be shared.

Even if you are not familiar with Lao Tzu's *Tao Te Ching* you may have heard one of the most famous and frequently quoted verses from the book: "The journey of a thousand miles begins with a single step." This brief passage inspired me to take the single step of creating a wisdom text focused on death. The journey toward greater acceptance of death in our society has many thousands of miles yet to proceed, but this book represents one small motion in that direction.

HOW WAS THIS BOOK WRITTEN?

Since I cannot read Chinese, I consulted 5 different English translations of the *Tao Te Ching* in order to grasp as nearly as possible Lao Tzu's original intention for his writing. I then meditated on each verse from the perspective of death in order to "see" how Lao Tzu's words could be applied to that subject. I repeated the process of reading and meditating many times for each passage until it became clear how to expand or reframe the verse in a meaningful way. Thus this book is an adaptation of the *Tao Te Ching* and should not in any way be considered a direct translation of Lao Tzu's words.

HOW MIGHT THIS BOOK BE HELPFUL?

The best way to use this book is to read just a little at a time, perhaps one verse each day. Let the words settle into your mind and touch your heart. Find your own meaning within the metaphors and paradoxical phrases. This book will introduce you to the practice of thinking about death every day and by the time you have finished all 81 verses you will have developed a new habit of death awareness. Your life will become richer with depth, meaning, joy and love as you learn to take nothing for granted and experience gratitude for every moment. You will feel calmer and less afraid of whatever the future holds for you.

It can also be helpful to keep a journal and record your thoughts about life and death each day as you study this book. You can download a free **Companion Journal** for *The Tao of Death* at www.eoluniversity.com/journal to assist you with specific writing prompts for each day, if you would like. The journal prompts are also recorded in the *Appendix* of this book.

WHAT IF YOU THOUGHT ABOUT YOUR OWN DEATH EVERY DAY?

This little book could change everything in your life! Indeed, it is my hope that ultimately our entire society will be transformed by the contemplation of death. As you read it, know that my desire is to share with you the peace of mind and heart that I have discovered through my own practice of death awareness. I honor your journey and send you much love "for the road." May *The Tao of Death* be a wise and informative companion for you, and may the rest of your life, no matter how long, be rich with love and joy and filled with wisdom and meaning.

With the deepest and highest regard,
Karen Wyatt MD

The Tao is the Way.
These verses are the Tao of Death,
written that you might live more fully
by embracing your mortality.

The Way of Death is also the Way of Life.
The two cannot be separated
for there is no Life without Death.
Life is the outward manifestation of All that exists,
while Death is the hidden inner essence of the All.
Just as Heaven becomes Earth
and Earth becomes Heaven,
the two are One.
Together Life and Death merge into the Great Mystery,
which is the secret of all existence.

Study Death in order to know Life.
When you learn the Way of Death
you will no longer fear the future.
When you live without fear
you will shine your light freely.

This is how you will change the world.

The Way of Death reveals the necessity of opposites.
Beauty can be appreciated because ugliness exists.
Virtue stands out in contrast to evil.
Simplicity is cherished in the midst of difficulties.
Starlight is only visible with the darkness of night.
Life is precious because Death is inevitable.

The two sides are intertwined and inseparable.
You cannot love one and reject the other.
Hold Life and Death together in the palm of your hand.
That is the Way of Death.

When you are no longer afraid of Death,
you will move through life effortlessly as you
perform deeds of compassion for all.
You will inspire others to live fully and
nurture everyone in your presence.
You will do great works without recognition
and change the world without saying a word.

The Way of Death teaches that

Love is what really matters.
He who lives according to Love
does not stir up disputes with others.
She who cherishes only Love
can never be robbed.
He who holds Love as the highest good
cannot be distracted by superficial things.

The Way of Death inspires a life of
clarity, integrity, humility, and wisdom.
Thus one who does not fear Death
creates order from chaos.

Death is infused in all of Nature
and is never exhausted.
Death is the origin of all Life,
complete and perfectly whole.
The Way of Death unites all beings
for it is shared by all of creation.
Those of all races, religions, nations, and creeds
are touched equally by Death.
Wealthy and poor, lowly and proud, miniscule and massive-
all beings are ultimately embraced by Death.

Both Life and Death are contained in every
drop of water,
breath of air,
blade of grass,
and particle of energy.

Death creates balance and harmony in the Universe
by arising in All that is
before and after
to infinity.

The Way of Death does not play favorites.

It gives Life to all things
and brings Death to all things.

Both good and evil,
darkness and light,
are treated equally as parts of one whole.

Life and Death cycle and flow continuously
and will never fail.

Words alone don't lead to an understanding of Death;
be still to comprehend its true essence.

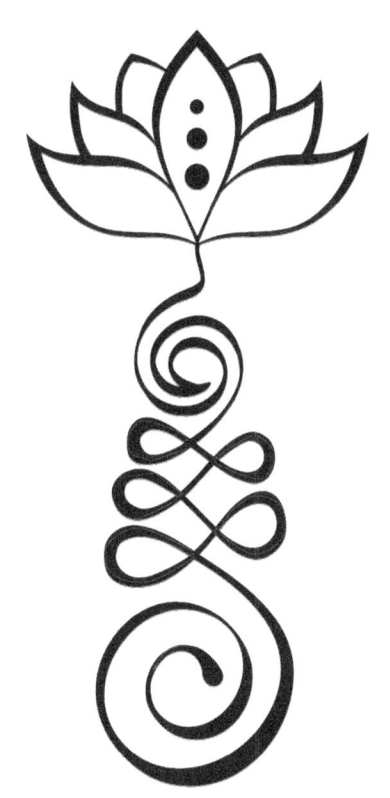

Death will never die.
Death is the pervasive root of all the Universe,
always with you;
always bringing new life.

When you come to know Death
you will find it to be the one thing
that will never fail you.

The Way of Death is infinite and will last forever.
Death desires nothing for itself
and therefore cannot be exhausted.

Death changes how we view everything about Life.
He who knows the Way of Death
leads by putting himself last,
succeeds by forgetting his own interests, and
fulfills his purpose by focusing on others.

Love is the greatest lesson
according to the Way of Death.
Love, like water, is
necessary for all of life
and adaptable to any space,
perfectly filling every gap and crevice.

Death teaches you to live according to Love,
with a mind that is calm and peaceful in its depth,
a heart that nourishes with kindness, and
words that flow with sincerity.
Let your love be like water that even though gentle
can penetrate solid rock.

When you are not afraid of Death,
love can flow freely and smoothly with the right timing,
impacting everything without really trying.
There is no need to force what is already moving.
Be like water.
Be Love.

The Way of Death teaches that
grasping for material wealth
eventually bankrupts the Soul;
striving for success
ultimately exhausts the life force;
seeking for approval
soon leads to bitterness.

Death advises:
focus not on illusions like wealth and success,
but turn your attention to what really matters.
Hold everything lightly in the palm of your hand
to find the path to serenity.

Can you see that the body and Soul are One
just as Life and Death are One?

Can you find peace and gentleness
within the suffering and Death you fear?

Can you love others just as they are?

Can you forgive everything that disappoints you?

Can you keep your focus on this present moment?

Can you be creative and nurturing
without needing to control?

Can you surrender your judgment
to the possibility of wisdom greater than your own?

Can you accept not knowing all the answers
to the questions of Life and Death?

In the Way of Death, these are the things
that really matter.

The Way of Death teaches that whatever has substance
must also have emptiness.
A wheel is useful only when it has a hole in the center.
A clay pot must be empty inside to hold wine or water.
A house can be inhabited only when it has space within.
A violin must be hollowed out before it can make music.

You too must be emptied in order to fulfill your purpose.

Death, and the thousand little losses it brings,
creates the emptiness needed for Life to flourish.

One who knows the Way of Death
is not obsessed with the sensory pleasures of life.
For colors, sounds, tastes, thoughts, and desires
create only fleeting moments of happiness.

Death teaches us to choose what really matters;
then we will discover the true depths of joy.

When you look at Life through the eyes of Death
it is equally foolish either to pursue fame
or to run away from rejection.
Both are concerns of the lower self and
neither really matters.

Likewise it is futile to fear Death
because you can't prevent it.
Death is only a threat to your physical existence.
Understand that there is something greater
than this body you inhabit
and this lower self that constricts you.
See the limitless Oneness that is
Death and Life combined.

Those who know the Way of Death
have no need to earn fame or to avoid rejection.
Be humble and grateful for who you are.
Do not fear the Death that makes Life fully possible.

Love the world and yourself infinitely and you will be able
to guide others away from fear's destructiveness.

What happens after we die?

The answer cannot be seen
or heard
or touched.
It remains a mystery
as deep as all darkness
without name
without form
beyond imagination.

The Way of Death
teaches you to live fully
within this mystery.
Simply be who you are,
right here, right now and
you will know all that you need to know.

Those who know the Way of Death
are both wise and mysterious.
Since they know that life is precious
they take care with every action,
allow time for things to unfold, and
have reverence for all living things.
They are simple, honest and open-minded;
able to surrender to the ups and downs of life.

Can you create peace in the world
with your inner calmness?
Can you find harmony with all beings
through your acceptance of everything that is?

When you learn to be unafraid of Death
you will be content with what you have
without being greedy.
You will embrace all that Life and Death offer to you
because of your humility.

Be still and contemplate this wisdom:
you know that everything in Nature
lives and flourishes for a time and
then returns peacefully to its Source.
You can witness this cycle of Life and Death
as it happens before your eyes.
This is the Way of Death
that governs all of creation.

Make peace with Death and
you can become enlightened.
Ignore Death and you will
wander in confusion and squander your days.

Accepting that you will one day die
allows you to open your mind and heart
under the guidance of your own intuition.
By knowing Death you know your Soul
and thus know God.

The Way of Death has been in existence forever,
before and after Time.

Some have always had an understanding of Death
without knowing how or why.
Others have learned to accept and appreciate Death
through the experience of Life.
But many have fear and hatred toward Death
because they lack faith in something greater than the self.

Everyone possesses this wisdom
deep within the Soul.
They would live with greater ease and harmony
if only they could be still enough to listen
to what they already know.

When we forget that Death is essential for Life,
we identify Death as the enemy.
We use artificial means to keep loved ones alive
long after their time to die.
Scientists create drugs and remedies to conquer Death,
fostering the illusion of immortality.

When families cannot talk about Death
they lose the opportunity to show true love.
When people do not prepare for Death
there is chaos at the end-of-life
and the medical system takes control.

The Way of Death teaches us to live
with integrity, intuition and love,
always mindful of Death as our companion.
Nothing else is needed.

There are many superficial teachings that obscure the Way
    of Death:

Exercise and follow a healthy diet in order to live longer.
Take supplements to prevent aging and death.
Trust doctors to prolong your life.

Yet none of these are as powerful as the Way of Death.
Live by these thoughts instead:

Make the most of each moment of life.
Be the best "you" you can possibly be.
Practice love above all else.

There are no guarantees.
Live each moment always wondering
if there will be another.
Let love of Life guide your choices rather than
fear of Death.

Knowing the Way of Death can free you from
worries and sorrow.
You could spend your time fretting about when to show
anger or respect,
or the difference between good and evil,
or all the fears that consume everyone else.

But when you are not afraid of Death
there's nothing else to fear.

Some people are controlled by their desires for more
possessions and forget to actually live their lives.
Some constantly seek excitement as if that makes life
worth living.
But these are all just distractions from the deep questions
of Life and Death.

When you do not fear Death you can be quiet and calm
like a baby who sleeps peacefully unaware of the world.
You may appear to others to be lost or simple or a fool.
To those who are bright and clever you may seem dull;
and while others are caught up in arguing
you will say nothing.

When you know the Way of Death
you can remain undisturbed like still water,
open-hearted and free like the wind.
Everyone else will believe they hold all the answers,
but you will possess true joy because you do not
fear Death.

It takes great courage to follow the Way of Death,
but those who do find comfort in its truth.
The Way of Death cannot be seen
or touched
or understood.
It requires faith and inner wisdom to trust that
Life has meaning even though Death is inevitable.

The Way of Death has been present since
before time and space.
All Life arises from Death.
This can only be known by embracing the Way of Death.

The Way of Death reveals itself through paradox:

When you accept your flaws you become whole.
When you seem to be in error
you are actually on the right path.
When you feel empty you are in fact completely full.
When you feel most discouraged you will be renewed.
When you do without you will receive what you need.
When you embrace Death you will finally experience Life.

Those who do not fear Death set an example for all others.
Because they don't call attention to themselves
their light can be seen clearly.
Because they don't try to prove themselves
they can be trusted.
Because they aren't attached to their own
individual identities
they can be a mirror for others.
Because they don't force their personal agendas
everything they do is significant.

When the ancient wise ones said,
"Surrender is the path to attaining everything,"
they were not using empty words.

Only by living without fear of Death
can you become your best and highest self.

Know when to speak and when to be silent.
Be like the wind that blows for a time then stops,
or the rainstorm that comes and goes.
The laws of Nature allow for everything
to have a beginning and an ending.
Accept that you cannot change Nature.

If you open yourself to the Way of Death
then you can embody what really matters
and bring it to the world.
If you become enlightened
then you can use your higher vision
to shine light for humankind.
If you learn to live with loss
then you can help others accept the losses
that continually arise in the cycle of Life and Death.

If you do not fear Death
you can trust your own true nature.

Listen to your intuition
and everything will unfold as it should.

Those who strive to be at the top will soon fall.
Those who push to get ahead of others will not go far.
Those who praise themselves will tarnish their own image.
Those who insist they know everything
will be shown their ignorance.
Those who seize power over others
will have their weaknesses exposed.
Those who are attached to their accomplishments
will eventually fail.

The Way of Death reveals all pretenses and false beliefs
of the ego.

Those who do not fear Death let go of this foolishness and
shine with pure love from the Soul.

There is something greater than all the laws of Nature--
greater even than the Universe itself.
It exists outside of time,
perfect in its serenity, emptiness and wholeness.
It will never change and never die.
It is the source of all creation and all creativity.

We have no name for this infinite source and so we call it
The Way of Death.

The Way of Death exists within all things,
gives Life to all things, and
returns everything back to the original source.

The ancients say that there are four great powers
in existence:
the Creative Force,
the Universe,
the Earth,
and Humankind.

Humankind must yield to the laws of the Earth.
The Earth must yield to the laws of the Universe.
The Universe must yield to the laws of the Creative Force.
The Creative Force operates through the Way of Death.

Because we have felt the heaviness of our burdens,
we can appreciate the lightness of our freedom.
Because we have experienced anxiety,
we can enjoy the presence of tranquility.
Because we understand Death
we can fully live Life.

One who follows the Way of Death is not fooled
by wealth or power or desire.
She is always at home within herself
no matter how far she travels.
She can live simply and wisely because
she knows what really matters.

This is the gift offered to us by Death.

Sacred work leaves nothing undone.
Sacred writing conveys a complete message.
Sacred intention considers the needs of all.
When we operate from our highest selves,
we don't need plans or orders or rules to tell us what to do.

A true Master reaches out to everyone and rejects no one.
One who knows the Way of Death
finds wisdom in everything and leaves nothing out.
This is what really matters.
This is enlightenment.

Those who are enlightened are teachers
for those who cannot see;
and those who cannot see bring lessons
for their enlightened teachers.
In this way, each of us is both a student and a teacher.
Therefore we should honor and value one another.

Some lessons are painful
but they contain the most wisdom.
Those who haven't learned this yet
are missing one of the fundamental secrets of life.

Be informed by the masculine perspective on life
but allow feminine wisdom to guide your behavior.
By receiving all that life has to offer,
like the river opens its embrace to all streams,
you will move through the world
with the innocence of a child.

Cherish all that is filled with light
but honor the darkness as well
to show the world how to cope with difficulty.
By being such a role model for the world
you will embody the Way of Death
and fulfill your highest purpose.

Celebrate all of your victories
but remain humble.
Be like the river valley that lowers itself
to carry even more of the water of life.
Humility will be your greatest asset along
the Way of Death.

Be like a simple piece of wood
that can be split and hollowed
to form tools and instruments.
Allow your suffering to shape you
then your life will be of the greatest service
for the good of all.

The Way of Death teaches this:
if you wish to have control over life
you will not be successful.
Life is a sacred mystery that
cannot be controlled or held onto.
If you try to force life to fit your plans
you will ruin it.
If you try to keep life in your grasp
you will destroy its meaning.

Understand that everything in the Universe
has its own flow and everything is in balance.
There will be times when you are the leader
and times when you are a follower.
In some situations you will feel strong and capable
and in others you will be confronted with your weaknesses.
Some accomplishments will come to you easily
and others will never be fulfilled despite your hard work.
On some days you will rejoice in the beauty
of life on planet Earth
and on other days you will weep at the suffering
and pain of humanity.

If you are wise you will follow the middle road
instead of rushing to one extreme or another.
You will not squander life's precious resources
but live in harmony and humility at all times.

This is the Way of Death.

Those who know the Way of Death
do not try to bend or twist the flow of life with force,
for that is futile behavior.

Trying to impose your will on the unfolding of life
leads to misery and unhappiness.
For when too much control is exerted
life itself is suffocated.

The wise one who follows the Way of Death
knows when to work and when to rest.
By understanding the cycle of life he has respect for
the Birth and Death of all things.
There is no need for self-promotion,
arrogance,
or force.
He understands that life must flow on its own terms
and embraces all that unfolds.

To fight a war against Death
is a foolish venture.
Those who know the Way of Death
will avoid such a battle.

Fear is the driving force behind
all desperate attempts to eliminate Death.
But a person governed by fear
does not grasp the higher wisdom of the Way of Death.
Calmness is the path toward healing.
Fear leads only to more fear and more fighting.

The paradox of the Way of Death is this:
When you run from Death
you will not enjoy Life.
When you accept Death as essential to Life
you will find the secret to fulfillment.
Mourn when those die who have not lived fully;
but be at peace when Death claims those
who have calmly lived every moment.

The Way of Death,
though it cannot be seen or held,
is the most powerful force in the Universe ...
and the simplest.

Those who understand the Way of Death
can become leaders for the entire planet.
They can show the way to harmony, balance
and sweetness on Earth without force,
by simply allowing the flow.

Though you may create institutions and systems
and give them names that sound important,
none of them will last because
they are not what really matters.
Know when to hold on and
when to let go of these finite creations.

All paths ultimately lead to the Way of Death
just as all streams eventually travel to the sea.

To understand other people is to have wisdom,
but to understand yourself is to attain enlightenment.
Dominating others requires sheer strength,
but controlling yourself is the true measure of power.

When you recognize that you already have what you need
you will see that you are indeed wealthy.
When you move through life with faith that all is well
you will manifest your true purpose.

When you embrace the Way of Death
you will live fully throughout your life.
And when the physical body dies
you will rejoice as you realize your own infinite nature.

The Way of Death is infinite and permeates everything.
All of Life depends on Death for its existence
but Death is humble and works behind the scenes.

Though the Way of Death is all-powerful
it waits patiently to be recognized.
Death ultimately provides love and nourishes all Life
yet has compassion for humankind's fear and rejection.

Death, in its greatness,
allows each person to awaken to it in her own time.

Embracing the Way of Death
is the great secret for living a life
of peace and happiness.

To those who are captivated by earthly delights,
the Way of Death may seem uninviting.
But they do not realize that Death is the mirror
that reflects the true beauty of Life.

While Death itself cannot be seen, heard or exhausted,
it enables us to enjoy fully all the music and food
and other fleeting pleasures
that will one day pass away.

To live by the Way of Death
you must give up your perception of
how things work:

Many situations grow worse
before they begin to improve.
Fever reaches a peak
before it breaks.
Illness becomes unbearable
before healing begins.
Chaos disrupts everything
before a breakthrough occurs.

Let go of control over your difficulties and
risk that they will grow worse.
Whatever you hope to attain
be willing to live without.
That is the secret to finding peace.

The Way of Death teaches
the power of paradox:
how kindness defeats toughness,
weakness overpowers strength,
and Death is essential for Life.
But keep this knowledge hidden in your heart −
let your actions reveal the truth.

Death is present within all things
though it is often hidden and can be overlooked.

If leaders and teachers understood the Way of Death
they could transform everything in this world.
To live the Way of Death is to live simply
and according to the laws of Nature.
Then everything would remain in balance
and there would be enough for everyone.
If everyone had what is needed then
there would be no grasping for more.
When there is no grasping each one would be at peace
and the world would exist in harmony.

Death is the greatest teacher of all,
showing the way to peace and equanimity
by letting go of all things that don't really matter.

Stop blaming Life for the troubles it has given.
Stop blaming Death for the joy it has taken.
Find joy within your troubles
and celebrate every precious moment.

The Soul behaves with goodness
because goodness is the Soul's nature.
The ego can only pretend to be good
and therefore cannot act with true goodness.
The Soul is naturally kind to all beings
but the ego must pretend to be kind.
The Soul behaves with fairness, honesty, and empathy
without even trying--they are part of the Soul's nature.
One whose actions are inspired by the Soul
is a peacemaker who connects with everyone.

The Way of Death teaches that
the ego must surrender to the Soul, which is eternal.
For when the ego rules:
genuine goodness is lost,
kindness disappears,
and peace is disrupted.
Then fear of Death becomes rampant and
humankind turns to science and religion
to create an illusion of immortality.
Thus the ego creates chaos.

Therefore, one who follows the Way of Death
allows the ego to be stripped of its pretenses
so that the Soul can guide with genuine goodness
that serves the wellbeing of all.

This is the nature of the Way of Death.

The Way of Death has existed since the beginning of time
and all of the Universe reveals its qualities.
The sky contains both light and darkness.
Stars are born and eventually die.
The planets orbit with balance and harmony.
Nature reveals the abundance of Life
that is nourished by Death.
Great teachers who know the Way of Death
bring much-needed wisdom to the world.

Without the cycle of Life and Death
none of this would exist.
The sky would be forever black,
the stars would burn out,
planets would implode,
Nature would become extinct,
and humankind would vanish.

Remember that all of the Life that we cherish
exists because of the Death of something else.
Life is built upon a foundation of Death.
Thus the truly wise are humble,
understanding that there is no greatness without Death.
Wholeness, health and true wealth
must embrace Death as an essential part.
The one who knows the Way of Death
values the common stone even more
than the polished jewel.

Life emerges from and returns to Death;
this cycle is ultimately the Way of Death
and it operates through surrender.

Everything in the Universe arises from
the Way of Death
as fullness emerges from emptiness
and substance comes from nothingness.

Dying is just this:
dissolving gradually into Love.

A person of expanded consciousness sees the
Way of Death as truth and immediately embraces it.
One who is still awakening admires the Way of Death
but cannot live by it.
Those who have not awakened at all view
the Way of Death as pure foolishness
and reject it.
The fact that they reject it reveals
that it is the true Way of Death.

This is the paradox of the Way of Death.
What is simple appears confusing.
Forward progress seems to be backward motion.
What is life-affirming looks threatening.
Strength appears to be weak.
Compassion seems foolish.
Integrity looks shameful.
Thus the most enlightened person can seem naïve
and one who lives by the Way of Death
may appear feeble and powerless.

The greatest skyscraper has a hidden foundation.
Beautiful music has an impact beyond sound.
Magnificent art touches the Soul in unseen ways.
So too, the Way of Death is mysterious and
operates in secret,
but gives life to everything
and makes everything whole.

Everything arises from One source,
but on Earth all things are perceived as opposites:
light and dark,
good and evil,
yin and yang,
feminine and masculine,
birth and death.
Thus One becomes two.

You are always choosing
one side or the other,
but there is a third way of seeing:
when opposites are integrated,
a new harmony is created.
Thus the fear of Death merges with the
wonderment of Birth
to produce love of Life.

This is the great secret of the Way of Death:
embrace Death to live the fullest Life.
For though the body fades away
the Soul belongs to the whole universe.
Without this knowledge life is meaningless
and death--nothing but a cruel destroyer.

For those who do not fear Death
compassion is more powerful than knowledge;
loving presence alone can penetrate a tightly closed heart.

From this it is clear that words are not necessary and
the most effective actions are those without expectations.
The true healer faces Death calmly and fearlessly,
and thus transforms illness into a sacred path.

If you can do your work in this world silently
and without attachments to the outcome
you will be a rare teacher
whose presence is desperately needed.

One who does not fear Death
embraces a new definition for success.

Would you rather be famous and known by everyone
or have a deep inner knowledge of yourself?
Would you rather have a great deal of material wealth
or be rich with spiritual wisdom?
Would you rather accumulate every possession you desire
or learn to let go of everything you don't need?

Focus on being content with what you have
and managing the excesses of ego;
you will live a fulfilled life and
have endless energy for bringing love to the world.

Things are never the way they seem from the outside.

The most amazing accomplishments
can appear insignificant.
A hollow instrument looks empty
yet fills an entire room with sound.
A straight path appears crooked.
Outstanding talent seems elementary.
Deep meaning hides behind simple words.
Death appears to be the loss of everything
but is actually the attainment of wholeness.

One who follows the Way of Death
knows when to move and when to be still.
Recognize that you can change the world
by being perfectly quiet.

When society understands the Way of Death
there is no futile attempt to prolong life and
no harsh treatments to wage a war with Death.
Life is celebrated and fully embraced
when there is harmony with Death.

Clinging too desperately to life causes suffering.
Fearing the ups and downs of life results in unhappiness.
Desiring immortality leaves life unfulfilled.

All of these false paths can be avoided
by finding contentment with life just as it is
and receiving Death whenever it arrives.

If you search outside of yourself for answers
to life's mysteries
you will never find them.
You can study great books and gather vast knowledge
but still the answers will not be revealed.

Everything you seek resides within you.
The answers are part of your own true nature.
Without searching or studying or striving
you already know that life is fleeting and precious.
You already know the Way of Death.

When you actively seek knowledge about life and death
you fill your mind with facts and data and information.

But when you learn the Way of Death
you empty your mind of all the things that
don't really matter.
When you give up trying to control life
you will be able to accomplish anything.

You can change the world
by letting go of your expectations.

The wise teacher knows what really matters.
She can relate to anyone
of any belief or level of consciousness.

She treats all people with kindness
whether they themselves are kind or unkind.
That is the true nature of kindness.

She extends her trust to everyone equally
whether they are honest or deceitful.
That is the true nature of trust.

She can find meaning in every event of life
whether joyful or painful.
That is the true nature of the Way of Death.

The wise teacher finds a way to connect with everyone
even though no one understands how she does it.
But they want to learn from her because
she is comfortable with both Life and Death.

Life and Death are both realities of this existence.
The Way of Death teaches that they are actually
two sides of the same coin.

But some people fear Death so much that
they cannot enjoy Life.
Others cling to Life so desperately that
they do not prepare for Death.
Still others disregard both Life and Death
and squander their days.

The few travelers who understand the Way of Death
are able to live Life fully while also embracing
the reality of physical Death.
They don't fool themselves
or hide from the truth.
Because they are free of expectations and fear
they flow through the ups and downs of life
with ease and harmony.

Love--the Creative Energy of the Universe--
gives rise to everything
and then draws it back again
with perfect timing.
This is the Way of Death.

Love breathes life
into material form
and nurtures, teaches, and protects it,
asking nothing in return,
until life dissolves once again
into Love.

Knowing that your life is just
a single breath of Love,
cherish everything
cling to nothing.

The Way of Death
whispers in your ear:
"There is only Love."

The Way of Death existed before time
and gave birth to the entire Universe.
Study Nature to understand the cycle of Life and Death:
all physical forms die but the Creative Energy of Love
is eternal.

If you do not know the Way of Death
you will cling to every desire and pleasure external to you,
fearing what the future holds.

If you know the Way of Death
you will let everything that touches you
slip through your fingers with ease,
and simply breathe in the present moment.

Understanding the Way of Death
allows you to see everything with clarity
and have the strength to live gently on this Earth.
Let the light that shines within you
illuminate your path through the struggles of life.

This is true enlightenment.

Once you learn the Way of Death
you will be motivated to stay on this path
and focus on the things that really matter.
But most people don't know this and
choose detours instead.

Thus there is corruption wherever you look.
Some pursue wealth and material possessions
while depriving others of a living wage.
Some stuff themselves with expensive food
while children go hungry.
Some seize power over others to
reinforce their need for control.
Some waste the precious moments of Life
to hide their own fear of Death.

Wake up and learn the Way of Death!
Face your fear and choose only Love.

54

When you know the Way of Death
that knowledge will never fail you
and can never be taken from you.
It will become your legacy one day.

If you want to make a positive impact on the world
begin by looking inside yourself.
If you live according to what really matters
then your family will overflow with love;
your community and nation will thrive;
and the entire planet will benefit
from the peace and goodwill that you generate.
You cannot change anything outside of you
until you change what is inside of you.

When you are not afraid of Death
you can let go of everything
that doesn't serve you or the world.

You will know this is true when
you understand the Way of Death.

One who lives according to the Way of Death
has the innocence of a newborn child and
is not swayed by the darkness that exists in this world.
Such a Master can be strong and gentle at the same time,
potent and passionate about life,
yet simple and pure;
able to radiate the truth consistently
without becoming exhausted
by all of the hatred and pain in the world.

The Master who knows the Way of Death
does not get too excited by external things
or overthink any situation.
He lives in harmony with Life and Death
letting all things come and go in their own time.
He understands that when all physical life
eventually perishes,
only Love will remain.

Those with true wisdom don't need to speak about it.
Talking too much is a sure sign of knowing nothing.

Say only what really matters,
keep to yourself,
soften your hard edges,
untie the knots of resentment you carry,
shine your light on your own Shadow,
and clean out all your hidden corners.
Do your own inner work first--
that is how you become aligned with the Way of Death.

Only then can you become a teacher for the world.
You will connect with everyone you meet
and they will long to be near you
even though you don't put yourself on display.
You will need nothing more and be at peace
with the ups and downs of life.

Like the Way of Death,
when you surrender everything
you will have exactly what you need.

When you understand the Way of Death
you can be a leader for others
by doing very little.
In fact you will be most effective
when you stop trying to control everything.

Consider this:
Too many rules can inhibit creativity.
Too much defensiveness leads to less safety.
Too much control results in confusion.
Too many laws produce more lawbreakers.
Too much medical care leads to more sickness.

The Way of Death teaches that everything
begins and ends with its own perfect timing.
A wise leader, therefore:
does only what really matters
and people transform in their own way;
says very little and people experience breakthroughs;
lets go of control and people do the right things;
asks for nothing and people embrace simplicity;
offers love and people heal their own sicknesses.

When you travel through Life
without fearing Death,
your equanimity calms the entire planet.

When your mind is open to new possibilities
your creativity thrives and you are free to be your true self.
But when your mind is filled with rigid rules
you become a false self who tries to please others.

The manifest world works like this:
Light depends upon darkness to make it visible.
Blessings are only apparent against the backdrop of tragedy.
Darkness and light are intertwined.
Death makes Life precious.
This is how it has always been.
What appears to be true can turn out to be false.
When we think we are doing good
we can actually be doing harm.
This confusion cannot be explained by the human mind.

The Way of Death teaches that everything--
whether black or white, good or bad in appearance--
is part of the whole of creation.
Nothing is left out; nothing is wrong.

Therefore the wise one walks the middle path.
Be virtuous without being judgmental.
Be consistent without being controlling.
Be honest without being cruel.
Be brilliant without boasting.
Live life to the fullest without ignoring Death.

When you follow the Way of Death
you focus on the things that really matter
because you understand that life is precious.
Rather than being ruled by the fickle desires of the ego
you enjoy the simple beauty of nature,
the presence of love,
the blessing of waking up to each new day.

With this awareness as your foundation
you can accomplish anything.
You are on the path to enlightenment.
By embracing whatever difficulties life brings to you
you can lead others through their own suffering,
which is the most profound blessing
you can offer to this world.

Just as food should be cooked gently without over-stirring,
life should be allowed to unfold
without too much meddling or control.

If you live according to what really matters
you won't need to worry about preventing
bad things from happening.
When you are in harmony with the Way of Death
then whatever comes your way
is an experience to be embraced,
your next opportunity for learning.

This is the best way to minimize evil in the world:
be in harmony in everything you do in your own life.

If you want to achieve greatness during your lifetime
become like the ocean.
This vast and powerful body of water
lies below everything else on the planet
and all rivers flow into it.
Be humble and receptive like the ocean
and you will attract the blessings
of all who want to share in your serenity.

Learning the Way of Death leads to humility
for even the most powerful will die
along with the most downtrodden.
There is no difference.

Become like the ocean:
use your power to gather those who have scattered,
to protect those who are vulnerable,
to absorb the pain of those who are suffering.
Receive what life has to offer you with equanimity.
Embrace Death whenever it arrives.
That is the nature of true greatness.

The Way of Death is the most magnificent truth
for it includes everyone and everything.
Kind and unkind people are treated equally--
their behavior doesn't matter.
Even the planets and stars in the heavens
yield to the Way of Death.

This truth can inspire people to transform their lives
and become the best they can possibly be.
But those who never hear the truth are equally accepted,
those who reject the truth are forgiven,
and those who cannot live by the truth are welcomed.

Everyone is on an equal playing field
at the moment of Death.

All leaders and teachers would be better off
learning the Way of Death than
accumulating great power, wealth or knowledge.
This teaching has survived throughout time
because it allows for unlimited expansion of consciousness
yet doesn't leave out a single unenlightened being.
There is no greater truth than the fact
that everything will one day die.

The Way of Death reminds us:
Problems that seem huge from our perspective
are actually small within the entire universe.
Therefore don't overreact to situations.
Use the least force necessary.
Intervene as little as possible.
Be still and meet hatred with love.

Break every challenge into small, simple steps
and you can accomplish anything.
If you want to create peace in the world
start by finding peace within yourself.
If you want to save the environment
first create a loving environment in your own home.
If you want to help others at the end of their lives
begin by facing your own fear of Death.

Wise ones don't tackle big problems all at once.
They seek the least complicated course of action
so they don't get discouraged or burned out.

Instead of looking for an escape,
accept that life is hard
and face your challenges step-by-step.
Get familiar with Death a little at a time,
then when it knocks on your door one day
you will greet it like a welcome friend.

In the cycle of Life and Death
everything has a beginning and an ending.
Tend to issues as they are beginning
and you will avoid bigger challenges later on.
Take good care of the tiny sapling
and it will grow into a sturdy tree.
Start with a strong foundation
and you can build a secure skyscraper on top.
Take the first step in the right direction
and you will have a successful journey.
Face your mortality early in life
and you will live fully before a peaceful death.

The key to life is to understand how to take action.
If you try too hard to control everything you will ruin it.
If you attach to a particular outcome
you will be disappointed.
Wise ones let go of control and the outcome
and find peace in their lives.

Don't let fear overcome you as the end of life approaches.
Stay calm and love each moment as much
as you did at the beginning.
Then you will find peace in your Death.

The wise ones remember that no knowledge,
material goods, or earthly pleasures
will lead to fulfillment at the end of life.
They spend their time
letting life unfold in its own way,
helping others to be their true selves,
and bringing as much love as possible to the planet.
This is the Way of Death.

There are different ways of knowing what is true.
You can gather knowledge from books
but your intuition also tells you what you need to know.
Too much book-learning makes life more complicated;
the mind sees everything as a confusing problem.
Today's difficulties can only be addressed
by allowing intuition to guide the intellect.

Too much education leads us to believe that
Death is a problem to be overcome.
But intuition teaches that all answers
arise from embracing Death.

In this paradoxical reality of the Way of Death
we have seen that what is greatest
is willing to take the lowest position,
as the ocean lies below the elevation of the river.

Therefore the greatest leader
is willing to become a humble servant.
She knows that yielding
is the secret to true strength,
just as Death is the secret to Life.
This kind of leader changes the world
without harming a soul.

Some believe the Way of Death doesn't matter--
focus on Life, they say, and ignore Death.
But Death makes Life precious
and gives meaning to existence.
Death cannot be ignored.

There are three essential lessons from the Way of Death
that can change how you see everything:
Love, Presence, and Surrender.
Love - to care for others unconditionally
and thus heal their wounds.
Presence - to be content with what exists in this moment
and live life fully.
Surrender - to let go of expectations for the future
and be in the flow of Life and Death.

Let Death teach you what matters
if you hope to become a leader.
Begin by cultivating these three things:
Love, Presence and Surrender.
You will be blessed and bless the entire planet.

Those who know the Way of Death
understand the art of balance.
They have discovered that power is found
within the tension between opposites,
just as Life exists between Birth and Death.
They find their balance on the middle path.

Thus the greatest leader exhibits a balance
between confidence and humility.
The enlightened spiritual teacher lives in balance
between compassion and discipline.
The true healer works with the balance
between science and mystery.

The middle path is the way to peace
because it makes room for every point of view.
Seek the middle path as you balance
between Birth and Death.
That is the secret of living fully
and dying peacefully.

There is a secret strategy for dealing with an enemy:
Be patient and don't make hasty decisions,
for it is better to yield than to be overly aggressive.

But the Way of Death teaches this:
your enemy is actually a mirror for your own Shadow,
offering you a chance to heal your wounds.
If you destroy the mirror
you destroy your opportunity to evolve.

So too illness and Death arrive in the guise of an enemy
though they are actually messengers
to help you learn and grow.
Before you attack and seek to eliminate the messenger
make sure you've heard the message.

To ignore the value of Death and its companions--
illness, suffering and loss--
is to dismiss your own potential for transformation.

True healing comes to the one who remembers
the three essential lessons of the Way of Death--
Love, Presence and Surrender--
and sees no one as an enemy.

The Way of Death is not hard to understand
if you don't overthink it.
It's not hard to practice
if you don't try to control everything.

Death comes for everyone
whether they have prepared for it or not.
That's a simple fact, as old as time.
Yet most people don't understand it
because they avoid thinking about Death.

If you want to learn the Way of Death
just look deeply inside your own suffering.
You'll find a precious gem
hidden within its distressing disguise.

Life and Death,
health and illness--
they're each a mystery and we will never know
all the answers.
It is far better to admit that we don't know
than to pretend that we know everything.

Be cautious if a practitioner tells you
he has answers for you.
Instead choose the healer who's not afraid to say
"I don't know."
That's the courageous person you want next to you
as you face an uncertain future.
The wisest among us recognize that they do not know.

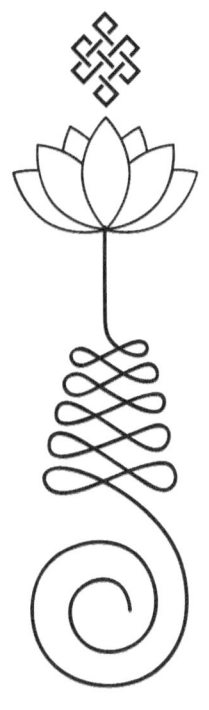

When people forget what really matters
they turn to superficial things to find meaning.

But each person must be allowed to follow her own path
both in her work and personal life.
Everyone is welcome in the Way of Death
whether they have awakened or remain asleep.

For this reason the true teacher
will never force an agenda on a student
or seek personal glory.
He knows well his own strengths and weaknesses
and can let go of everything else
while keeping to what really matters.

Is it better to courageously fight
against an illness that leads to Death;
or to focus on living life fully and allow
Death to take its natural course?
There is no one answer to that question
because each person must find his own way of
living and dying.

The Way of Death has no specific plans for anyone
but accepts everyone and every path.
The Way of Death doesn't preach any dogma
yet you will find your own answers within it.
The Way of Death doesn't make any promises
yet you will have what you need.
The Way of Death always flows spontaneously
yet is connected to everything.

Death is the ultimate "safety net."
It covers the entire universe and
lets nothing fall through.

Some are not afraid of Death
and cannot be manipulated through their fears.

But others do fear Death
and spend their lives doing everything possible
to prevent what is going to happen anyway.

The Way of Death is universal and necessary
for Life to exist.
If you try to stop Death
you will only bring harm to yourself
for that power is not meant for your hands.

When the ego is in charge of your life
it governs through greed, judgment, and fear.

Greed drives the pursuit of material wealth
and leaves the Soul starving.

Judgment hinders creativity
and the Soul cannot express itself.

Fear leads to avoidance of Death
and the Soul cannot flourish.

The ego tries to control life
but the Soul takes everything lightly
without greed, judgment or fear.

Thus the Soul animates life to the fullest
while the ego crushes life
in its desperate grasp.

In the cycle of Life and Death
all things are soft and supple at birth--
like a newborn baby or a tiny sapling--
and become stiff and hardened before death.
So flexibility is a sign of life
while rigidity is a sign of death.

The ego creates rules that are hard and fast
while the Soul is infinitely adaptable.
When the ego is in charge
every breeze can break you
like a brittle tree in a storm.
But when the Soul guides your life
you will bend easily with the winds of change.

The ego will one day die.
The Soul will exist for eternity.
The Way of Death helps you see the difference.

The Way of Death is like a drawn bow:
Life arises from the tension between Birth and Death
just as the bow's power derives from the taut string.

Perfect equilibrium is maintained
by adding or subtracting as needed.
Thus all of Nature is balanced
in the cycle of Life and Death
and the ecosystem sustains itself.

But human nature has forgotten the Way of Death
and operates by the greed and fear of the ego.
The greedy ones grasp for more and more
and deprive others of what they need.
The fearful ones seek to prolong life at all costs
and deprive themselves of meaningful days.

Who manages to give to others and still live life fully?
Only those who know the Way of Death.
They don't focus on living a longer life.
They infuse every moment with meaning,
right here, right now.
They don't cling to superficial glory
or seek recognition for their actions.
They go about their work quietly and with humility
so no one notices that they are saving the world.

Water is the most miraculous element on Earth,
infinitely adaptable and powerful at the same time.
It can change its shape to follow any narrow pathway,
nurture the tiniest sprout in the garden,
destroy entire coastlines with its force,
and carve vast canyons with its persistence.

The Way of Death reminds us to be like water:
adapt to whatever challenges come along,
care for others who need nurturing,
take bold action when necessary,
and work without attachment to the outcome.
But almost no one can do it.

The wisest teachers are the ones who know
that our suffering shapes our transformation,
and embracing Death is the path to a fulfilled Life.
This wisdom is paradoxical but true.

When the ego rules our negotiations with others
there will always be resentment
because any compromise seems unfair.

So rise above the ego's greed
and operate from the Soul:
in every situation treat others with generosity
and expect nothing in return.

This is how Death operates:
it favors no person over another
and nourishes every life.

Those who embrace it find peace and contentment
no matter what happens.

Learn to be content with what you have.
Expand your consciousness as much as possible
but return always to a simple way of life.
Thus your Soul becomes vast
but your day-to-day life remains small and manageable.

The Way of Death teaches you to focus on
what really matters.
Instead of searching for contentment in other places
grow your own satisfaction where you live right now.
Instead of building walls for protection from others
build bridges and find common ground with everyone.
Instead of squandering your money on flashy possessions
cherish simple things that remind you who you really are.

Make the most of every moment of life
and be fully present at all times.
Eat delicious food, wear your favorite clothing,
read an inspiring book, relax in your own home,
and find practices that enlighten you.

By filling each moment with meaning--
whether you are rich or poor,
famous or unknown,
well-traveled or homebound--
you will weave together a life filled with meaning.
Then when Death arrives you will be ready
to dissolve effortlessly into the light.

The truth is often spoken in plain words
while lies can be hidden behind elaborate speech.
One who knows the truth doesn't need to argue.
Those who insist on their own correctness
are missing the truth altogether.
The ego demands attention for its knowledge and
    education
while the Soul quietly acts upon the truth
without saying a word.
All the education in the world can't teach you the truth.
Therefore the most intellectual person may know nothing
while a simpleton totally grasps what is true.

The Way of Death is the truth.
Those who know it live by these principles:
Stop trying to accumulate possessions
and you will have everything you need.
Give freely to others
and you will become spiritually rich.
Embrace Death
and you will find meaning in Life.

The Way of Death
brings about the highest good for all of creation.
Be wise like that:
be the best person you can be
and bless the world with your gifts.

May you find the secret to love and joy
by contemplating the mysteries of
Life and Death.

Karen Wyatt

SOURCES

1. Mitchell, Stephen. *Tao Te Ching: A New English Version*. Harper Perennial, 1991.

2. Heider, John. *The Tao of Leadership*. Bantam New Age, 1986.

3. Lin, Derek. *Tao Te Ching: Annotated and Explained*. SkyLight Illuminations. 2006.

4. Feng, Gia-Fu and Jane English. *The Complete Tao Te Ching*. Vintage Books, 1989. Web. 20 June 2016. http://terebess.hu/english/tao/gia.html

5. Unknown translator. *Tao Te Ching*. World I-Kuan Tao Organization. 15 March 2016. http://www.with.org/tao_te_ching_en.pdf

APPENDIX

The Tao of Death
Companion Journal

The journal prompts on the following pages have been created to help you develop a practice of death contemplation, which we have seen can enrich your life overall. As you read the verses in *The Tao of Death* remember that the meaning may not be clear to you initially. As you write about them you will gradually find greater clarity in these words.

By choosing to complete these prompts you are taking the first step toward greater awareness of the realities of Life and Death AND ensuring that you will experience less fear and more peace as you approach your own later days of life.

Each prompt in this journal is paired numerically with the corresponding verse in **The Tao of Death**. You might want to read one verse each day and journal about that verse, using the suggested prompt for guidance. The choice is yours: you can proceed through the verses in numerical order or randomly—whatever fits your needs the best.

By spending a little time each day contemplating Death and

its importance for Life, you will be increasing your own appreciation for the fleeting nature of existence. This daily practice will soon bring you the rewards of greater joy and less fear as you learn to be present and fully engaged in all of Life.

**You can also download a print version of
The Tao of Death Companion Journal
at this webpage:**

Eoluniversity.com/journal

The Tao of Death
Companion Journal

1. The study of Death forces you to look at your deepest fears. What do you fear most?

2. Life consists of both "good" and "bad" experiences, which provide balance and contrast for one another. What aspects of life do you reject? How do they help you appreciate what you love about life?

3. Death focuses attention on what is most important in life. What do you value most in your life?

4. Death is a necessary part of life. How has death touched your life up to this point?

5. Contemplate the necessity of death in nature. How does your own existence depend upon the death of other beings?

6. Death is inevitable. What would you like to know about it?

7. Death can change everything in your life. Where are you resisting change right now?

8. Death teaches us to slow down and allow life to unfold. What are you trying to force into existence in your life? Where do you need to slow down?

9. Death erases all illusions. How do your desires for wealth and success dictate your actions and control your decisions for life?

10. When you think about death what fears arise within you? Can you recognize anything positive about death?

11. How has your life been "emptied" in the past? What have you lost?

12. The pleasures of life are not the same as true joy. When have you been able to experience joy even when pleasure is absent?

13. Think about the possibility that some part of you will survive even after your physical body dies. Can you sense the presence of that part of you right now? What is it like?

14. Practice being in the present moment by taking 3 deep breaths and focusing only on the breath. Reflect on how you feel physically, emotionally, and mentally after this exercise.

15. Think about the fact that life is fleeting and yours could end at any moment. What is most precious to you if this is your last moment of life?

16. What expectations do you have for your life? How attached are you to those hopes and dreams?

17. When you think about the fact that you will one day die what emotions arise for you?

18. Do you follow your own inner wisdom or look to others for guidance? Practice listening for your own intuition by spending time in quiet contemplation each day.

19. What practices do you follow in order to stay healthy live a longer life? Are they motivated by fear or love?

20. What worries occupy your thoughts right now? When you think about the fact that you will die one day does it change how you see those problems?

21. What gives your life meaning right now? How would that change if you were told you had only a few weeks to live?

22. Think about the statement: Surrender is the path to attaining everything. What does that mean to you? What do you need to surrender in your life?

23. What losses are you coping with in your life right now? Can you see them as part of a natural cycle of life?

24. What are you striving to achieve in your life? How might you base your goals more on love than on accomplishment?

25. There are many "small deaths" that occur in a lifetime as we experience change and growth. What "small deaths" have occurred in your life to allow new things to arise?

26. How have the difficult times of your life helped you to appreciate the joyous times?

27. When have you been a student in your life and when have you been a teacher? Can you recognize that every person and every experience has something to teach you?

28. How has life has been shaping you through all of the difficulties you have experienced? How has your path been changed?

29. In what ways are you trying too hard to control life? What plans are you trying to force in your life that may not be working out as you wish?

30. What aspects of your life are flowing well and which are not? Where can you use more rest and less control in your life?

31. Do you know anyone who lives life to the fullest? What can you learn from that person? How might you enjoy every moment of life?

32. What are you clinging to in your life? Is it really important or do you need to learn to let it go?

33. In what way do you "already have what you need?" Are you content with what you have or longing for something more?

34. Why is this the right time for you to awaken to an understanding of Death?

35. Think of the fact that everything in your life is fleeting—what you have right now you may soon lose. How can you enjoy the little pleasures of life fully before they are gone? Choose at least one thing that you will make the most of today.

36. Think about a time of distress in your past. How did the situation grow worse before it improved? What can you learn now from that experience?

37. How might your life change if you felt satisfied with what you already have? How can be more content with things exactly as they are right now?

38. Are your actions generally guided by ego or by Soul? How can you tell the difference?

39. What aspects of your life are like "the common stone" and which represent "the polished jewel?" What do you value most?

40. Think back on your own life as part of the cycle of life and death. How can you find peace in your own journey from birth to your eventual death?

41. How has your life actually benefitted from the suffering you have endured in the past?

42. Write about the parts of your life that you have labeled as "good" or "bad." How can you embrace what appears to be negative and see it as part of the whole?

43. What does it mean to you to do silent work in the world? Where in your life can you be of service to others without being seen?

44. What is missing from your life? What will it take for you to feel content with what you have?

45. Think about all of the losses you have experienced in life thus far. How have they made you more whole?

46. Imagine that you have been told you have only a few weeks to live. How would you like to spend your days?

47. What questions are you seeking to have answered about your life? Reflect on the idea that the answers are already within you.

48. In what ways do you need to give up trying to control your life? What expectations are you clinging to?

49. Who are you unable to find a connection with? Who do you reject and why?

50. What does it mean to embrace the reality of physical death? How might this realization help you live more fully?

51. How might it be possible to cherish everything in your life without clinging to it?

52. How has your own path through difficulty led you to greater enlightenment?

53. Where have you taken detours in your life from the path of your Soul? Where has the ego been in charge?

54. What needs to change within you in order to have a positive impact on the world?

55. Have you been caught up with excitement about an event if life, only to be disappointed later? What would it take to view everything from a more neutral stance?

56. What resentments are you carrying with you from the past? Write about each one and how you can begin to let them go.

57. A recurring theme of the Way of Death is that "less is more." Where in your life might you do less or let go of some of your control?

58. "Blessings are only apparent against the backdrop of tragedy." What blessings can you find in the tragedies of your life?

59. As you recognize that life is precious, what simple things do wish to enjoy to the fullest today?

60. What is unfolding in your life right now? How can you step back from trying to control it and be at peace with whatever happens?

61. Where could you use a little more humility in your life?

62. Reflect on this thought: "Everyone is on an equal playing field at the moment of Death."

63. Think about a big task you are facing. How can you break it down into small, doable steps?

64. What fears do you need to overcome as you face the later years of your life?

65. What do you "know" within yourself that you have not learned from books? How can you listen more for this inner wisdom?

66. Where can you become more humble in your life? How could you lead others by being a servant to them?

67. How can you have more compassion toward others in your life? Choose three things you might do to develop your own capacity for compassion.

68. Think about the extreme polarization that exists in our society—political, cultural, economic, and philosophical. The middle path finds a way to embrace all diversity. Where do you see yourself fitting in and how could you get closer to the middle path?

69. What "enemies" have you identified in your life? How can you change your mindset to view them with more compassion, presence and surrender?

70. The suffering we experience during our lifetimes helps prepare us for our eventual dying process. What have you learned from suffering thus far in your life?

71. What answers do wish you had about your own health and illness? How can you live in greater peace without knowing those answers?

72. Draw a timeline of your own path of spiritual development. What experiences have led you to this point in life?

73. Think about the choices offered in this passage: fighting against an illness in hopes of prolonging life or allowing Death to come naturally, without a fight. What would you choose for yourself and why?

74. Examine your daily habits and activities. Are you doing any of them out of fear? How could you make love your motivation instead of fear?

75. This passage tells the difference between ego-driven and Soul-guided behaviors in life. When are your actions governed by greed, fear or judgment?

76. What changes in your life are you meeting with rigidity and stiffness? How can you become more flexible and "bend with the winds of change?"

77. How can you find deeper meaning in your life right here, right now?

78. This passage says: "Our suffering shapes our transformation." How has that been true in your life?

79. What do you expect to receive in return for your acts of generosity? How can you let go of those expectations?

80. What simple things can you emphasize in your life to make the most of every moment?

81. What gifts do you feel you have for the world? How can you offer those gifts more fully than ever before?

ABOUT THE AUTHOR

KAREN WYATT MD spent years as a doctor caring for patients in challenging settings, such as hospices, nursing homes and indigent clinics before she left medicine to pursue a new career as an author, speaker, and podcaster. She draws on her years of medical experience in the stories she includes in her narrative non-fiction books, which focus on the everyday spiritual lessons we all need to learn in order to live our best lives.

She is the host of the popular End-of-Life University Podcast and has inspired thousands of people to find love and joy in the midst of difficult times. Check out her website at
http://www.eoluniversity.com.

www.ingramcontent.com/pod-product-compliance
Lightning Source LLC
Chambersburg PA
CBHW020403130626
46549CB00006B/2422